DON'T STRESS!

How to Keep Life's Problems Little

Don't Stress!

How to Keep Life's Problems Little

Nancy E. Krulik

SCHOLASTIC INC.

New York   Toronto   London   Auckland   Sydney

ISBN 0-590-63271-X

12 11 10 9 8 7 6 5 4 3 2   8 9/9 0 1 2 3/0

Printed in the U.S.A.   40
First Scholastic printing, December 1998

For Ian.
I wish you peace and
happiness forever!

Contents

Introduction

1 • Stop Using Others As Your Mirror . . . It's How You View Yourself That's Important!

2 • The Sun Will Come Up Tomorrow . . . Unless, Of Course, It's Cloudy

3 • It's a Bad Hair Day . . . Try Wearing a New Hat!

4 • Pssst . . . Here's a Note

5 • Rise and Shine!

6 • Sometimes Being Right Can Turn Out Wrong (Or the Demise of the Words "I Told You So!")

7 • It's Only a Thing

8 • We'll Return to Our Show After This Commercial Message!

9 • Don't Let History Repeat Itself

10 • Find Your Hidden Talent

11 • Study!

12 • It's Just a Letter . . . Why Grades Don't Tell the Whole Story

13 • Remember: Even Paula Cole Couldn't Get a Date for Her Prom

14 • Start a New Trend

15 • What I Like About Me

16 • Mirror, Mirror, on the Wall

17 • Say Cheese!

18 • Stick Your Fingers in Your Ears . . .

19 • Spend an Afternoon Just Staring at the Clouds

20 • Listen to the Music in Your Head

21 • Congratulations to Me!

22 • Take Me to Your Leader

23 • Be the Teacher for a Change

24 • Make Every Day Thanksgiving Day

25 • Make It Worth the Wait

26 • Work for Peace

27 • Give Grandma a Call

28 • Brotherly (and Sisterly) Love

29 • Here's a Bonus!

30 • Have Great Fantasies

31 • Honesty Is the Best Policy . . . Honest!

32 • Have a Conversation With Your Dog (Or Your Cat, Your Hamster, Your Canary . . .)

33 • Rub a Rock

34 • Make Friends With Mother Nature

35 • Study the Stars

36 • Say "I Care"

37 • Call Time Out

38 • Don't Keep It to Yourself

39 • Learning to Listen

40 • First Things First

41 • Don't Let Others Bring You Down . . . and Don't Make Them Responsible for Bringing You Up, Either

42 • You're Not a Know-It-All

43 • The Land of the Brave

44 • Choose Your Battles

45 • Keep Your Eyes on Your Own Paper

46 • Play Mind Games

47 • "I Love Your Smile!"

48 • Try Being Two-faced

49 • Work Out!

50 • Be Prepared

51 • Don't Worry About Tomorrow

52 • For the Love of Leaves

53 • I Think I Can . . . I Think I Can . . .

54 • "Stay As Sweet As You Are"

55 • Surprise! I Choose You

56 • Weekly Run-through

Introduction

Grown-ups think that they've cornered the market on stress. But kids are under a lot of pressure, too. There's always tomorrow's spelling test, or the big softball game on Saturday, or your pesky little brother who's discovered your diary.

Life is full of tiny aggravations. The trick is not to let them get to you. Easier said than done? Not at all. It's just a matter of learning new ways to deal with the things that bother you most. And that's where this book comes in. Just stick with the tips in these pages. They'll help you stomp out the things that bug you!

Stop Using Others As Your Mirror . . .
It's How You View Yourself That's Important!

Isn't it weird how we care so much about what others think of us? We let people put us into all sorts of categories. You've heard the labels: the brains, the jocks, the nerds . . .

But no one really fits into a category. Foods fit into groups, people don't! So before you let someone else define you, remember: Each person is unique. And we are all made up of many different characteristics. The names other people give you can never define you — they can only confine you. Don't you let them!

The Sun Will Come Up Tomorrow . . . Unless, Of Course, It's Cloudy

Okay. So it's bedtime, and you realize that this has been, without a doubt, the *absolute* worst day of your life. Oh, well. Some days are like that. The key is to leave today in the past and remember that tomorrow is a brand-new day. Think of that new day as a clean sheet of paper. Only *you* can decide what is written on that empty page. It's up to you to scribble down words that are dismal and dull or bright and happy.

Do yourself a favor. Leave the clouds to Mother Nature. Fill all of your tomorrows with as much sunshine as you can.

It's a Bad Hair Day . . . Try Wearing a New Hat!

We all have days when we look a lot less than our best. But don't spend the whole day hiding in the bathroom. View those bad hair days as a challenge! Think of it this way: If your hair looks messy, it's the perfect time to wear that new funky, floppy hat you found at the vintage clothing store. And if you spill paint all over your new pants, don't freak out. Now you've started a new fashion trend!

With a little creativity, your style will shine through, giving you the confidence you need to make it through the day!

Pssst . . . Here's a Note

There's something *so* exciting about receiving a letter. It's the thrill of tearing open the envelope, carefully unfolding the paper, and reading the words on the page.

Putting pen to paper is a great way to tell a friend just how much he or she means to you. It gives you a chance to compose your thoughts and write what you really feel. Knowing that you've made someone's day better will lift your spirits as well.

Try writing at least one special friendship note a day. Just don't pass them during math class!

Rise and Shine!

"You're going to miss the bus! Don't forget to take your homework. Did you remember to make your bed?"

Let's face it. Morning is not exactly the most relaxed time of the day. If you're like most kids, getting ready for school is more like a mad dash through an obstacle course. You have to grab your books, wolf down your breakfast, and get out the door — avoiding arguments with your parents and siblings along the way.

The best approach to getting through the morning rush is to prepare the night before. Pack up your lunch and put it in the refrigerator. Leave your backpack by the front door. Lay out your clothes before you go to sleep. Finally, set your alarm clock for a half hour earlier than you normally get up.

You'd be surprised how much you can get done in that extra half hour. You may even find a few more minutes to practice for your piano lessons — before school! (That will give you time in the evening to watch that new show you've been dying to check out.) When your morning starts out smoothly, the rest of the day is sure to follow!

6

Sometimes Being Right Can Turn Out Wrong
(Or the Demise of the Words "I Told You So!")

Why is it so important that we be right all the time? It isn't. But we sure do put a lot of energy into being correct — and making sure that someone else knows he's wrong.

Many of life's questions have no real right or wrong answers. And most of us would be a lot happier is we stopped focusing on proving ourselves right — and started focusing on making ourselves happy. Just think of all the fun things you could do with the time saved by not arguing!

It's Only a Thing

"I can't believe you ruined my favorite sweater."
"How could you lose my favorite bracelet?"

We all form attachments to objects. Sometimes there's a sentimental value attached to items that makes them worth much more than their actual dollar value. In that case, what we're attached to is not the object but the emotion behind it. And *nobody* can lose or destroy that. And if it's the object itself you are attached to, just imagine breaking or ruining it *yourself* instead of your friend. Would you feel more forgiving? Remember: Objects can always be replaced. Friendships can't.

8

We'll Return to Our Show
After This Commercial Message!

Whenever you come face-to-face with what seems like a really bad situation, it's time to give yourself a new job: TV writer.

Most TV characters solve their problems in a matter of thirty minutes (twenty-two if you don't count the commercials!).

TV writers often come up with alternative endings for their shows. Write down all the different ways you can handle your problem. Some of your solutions will lead you into more stressful situations. But others will show you that there's a light at the end of the tunnel. That's the direction you'll want to follow.

Don't Let History Repeat Itself

No matter how many ways you find to avoid them, some problems do hit you head-on. And sometimes you will make mistakes in how you handle them. The key is to learn from your mistakes and vow not to make the same errors again. That way, as you deal with the consequences of your blunder, you can keep saying to yourself, "At least when this is all over, I'll never have to go through *that* again." Learn from your mistakes!

Find Your Hidden Talent

Nothing can make someone feel better than knowing he's good at something. Not necessarily the best, but awfully good. Everyone has a talent hidden somewhere inside them. The trick is finding what your talent is. Usually people are interested in the things they have a natural inclination for. So, if you love the sound of a guitar, take a few lessons and see how it goes. If you like the freedom of running fast, join the track team. Once you find your hidden talent, there's no stopping you! And you'll find that your confidence will take you to new heights!

Study!

Sorry, but that's the only real way to de-stress before a test. Naturally, you're going to do better in some subjects than in others. And you probably have a friend who does well in the classes you don't have a flair for. So maybe you can help each other reduce test stress — by studying together. You help her with the math and science, and she'll pull you through that spelling test. And you just may be surprised: Working together can actually make learning fun!

It's Just a Letter . . .
Why Grades Don't Tell the Whole Story

Let's face it. It would be nice to pick up your report card and see a list of A's staring back at you. But it doesn't always happen that way. And sometimes getting less than an A can be pretty disappointing.

The truth is, people put far too much emphasis on grades. School isn't for acquiring high averages. It's about learning. School is a place where you prepare for life as a grown-up. And just because you are not a great test taker, or raising your hand in class makes you nervous, doesn't mean you don't have a huge store of knowledge in your head — knowledge that is sure to come in handy someday.

More important than what your grades say is what your heart says. Do you go to school each day eager to gather new information? Do you try your hardest to study, pay attention, and do the work? Are *you* satisfied with your work? If you can answer yes to those questions, then you've got a 4.0 average where it really counts.

Remember: Even Paula Cole
Couldn't Get a Date for Her Prom

It's true! Pop sensation Paula Cole recalls not being able to get a date for her own senior prom. And look at her now!

You've got to remember that you are in this life for the long haul. The things that mean a lot to you now may not be all that important in the coming years. In fact, when you're going to your tenth high school reunion, no one is going to remember that you dropped your tray in the middle of the cafeteria, or that you started singing (off-key, of course) before anyone else in the choir. And since none of these little tragedies are going to matter in the long run, why not laugh them off now?

Start a New Trend

So you don't think those new T-shirts *everybody* is wearing will look good on you? And maybe those new platform shoes (on sale now!) are a little less comfortable for walking to and from school. Are you tired of following trends?

Before you go out and buy yourself something you know is totally wrong for you, ask yourself this simple question: Is it really *me*? All kinds of people will try to tell you what's right for you. But the only person who knows what style, color, and haircut work for you is *you*! So go out and buy what you like. And who knows — you may be the next trendsetter!

What I Like About Me

Imagine waking up every morning and discovering a list of all the things that make you great. Well, don't just imagine it . . . do it! Make a list of all the things you do well: Maybe you're a good friend, amazing at tennis, and helpful around the house. Be sure to list every single one of your most wonderful attributes. Then hang the list on your wall. And be sure to read it every morning before you leave your room to start the day.

Mirror, Mirror, on the Wall

Do you like yourself? You should! You're a one-of-a-kind special person — full of promise and possibilities.

So every morning, before you go off to face the world, look in the mirror and say, "I like myself!"

Watch your face as you say those words. A smile is sure to spread. In fact, it's practically impossible to say "I like myself" with a frown.

Say Cheese!

No matter how gray the day, put a sunny smile on your face. Your brain will begin to believe that you're happy. Don't believe us? Give it a try. It's a scientific fact that using the power of suggestion (in this case a smile) will help convince yourself that you really *are* happy. And before long, that smile will be the genuine article!

If that's not a good enough reason to grin, think of it this way: Smiling is relaxing. Your face uses far fewer muscles to smile than it does to frown.

Stick Your Fingers in Your Ears . . .

Okay, we don't mean *literally* stick your fingers in your ears. We mean no more eavesdropping!

When you overhear snippets of a conversation, you are liable to misunderstand the gist of what is being said. Suppose you hear two of your friends talking about a great party Friday night — a party you haven't been invited to. You're likely to feel hurt, left out, lonely, and frustrated. Of course, you missed the beginning of the conversation — the party is a surprise . . . for you!

Spend an Afternoon Just Staring at the Clouds

Life is so complicated. We're always running here, calling there, and trying desperately to get everything done in just twenty-four hours.

If you ever want to de-stress, stop whatever activity you are doing. Give yourself a chance to focus on absolutely *nothing*. Lying on your back and staring at the clouds is just the kind of relaxation your body is begging for. So stretch out and look at those white cottony puffs up there.

Just a few minutes of staring into space will do your brain and body a world of good. And when you're finished contemplating whether that cloud to the left looks more like an ice cream cone or a rocket ship, you'll be rested and ready to face the world with renewed energy and confidence.

Listen to the Music in Your Head

Do you have a favorite pop tune? Something upbeat and happy, with lyrics that make you want to dance or smile? Well, you can take that music with you wherever you go. Just play that song over and over again . . . in your head!

When you're walking down that street, think of your favorite song. Before you know it, you'll be stepping in time to the beat and smiling as you run through those happy words and that peppy tune. Music is a very powerful force. Let it lift you up!

Congratulations to Me!

Some people aren't confident about their talents until someone else recognizes them. They wait and wait and wait . . . for others to tell them they've done a good job.

But why wait? Deep down inside you know when you've gone that extra mile or achieved a goal you never thought you would. So instead of waiting for an outsider to recognize your talents, give yourself a pat on the back and say, "Congratulations to me!"

Take Me to Your Leader

The next time you feel like you've got HUGE problems, imagine you're an alien studying human behavior. Looking at your life from a space creature's point of view will help you see the big picture. You might realize that things are not as bad as they seem. More important, pretending that you are an alien is guaranteed to make you laugh. And humor is one of the best remedies for any problem.

Be the Teacher for a Change

Does your school have a peer-tutoring program? If it does, sign up. Teaching others is a great way to feel good about yourself. First of all, you'll have the satisfaction of making someone else's life a little easier. And who knows — you might even learn something! But most important, tutoring will give you the opportunity to make a new friend. And that is the greatest gift of all.

Make Every Day Thanksgiving Day

Have you ever had one of those days when you feel like you are the sorriest person in the world? A day when it seems like everyone else has an easy life and yours is the pits? Well — believe it or not — that's the perfect time to give thanks!

When you feel your lowest, that's the time to make a list of all the things in your life that you are thankful for. You can list the big things, such as family, friends, your dog, and having a roof over your head. But you should also list the little things that make life worth living, like the fact that your mom makes the most amazing strawberry French toast, that your dad loves playing one-on-one basketball with you on Saturdays, and that your little sister has ballet class after school so you'll get to listen to *your* music for a change.

Once you see how many wonderful things you have to be grateful for, you'll realize that your life is pretty great after all.

Make It Worth the Wait

Did you ever try to count up all the time you spend waiting in lines? There's the line in the cafeteria, the line at the movie ticket booth, the line at the checkout counter at the record store . . . well, you get the picture.

Waiting in line can get pretty frustrating — particularly if you're spending your waiting time thinking about all the things you need to do after you get to the front of the line. So don't think about them. Spend your line time trying one of these:

Isometric exercises. Place your palms together and push them against each other as hard as you can. It will build your muscles!

Imagine what all the people in line looked like as babies. You'll laugh your way up the line.

Imagine that you are a movie star stopping to pose for the paparazzi. Just keep those smiles and waves imaginary, too. Unless you *want* people to stare at you!

Work for Peace

After a long, hard day, it should feel nice to come home to your peaceful house and unwind. But for lots of kids, home is a war zone. Nobody wants to live in a place where there's constant fighting and screaming. So for the sake of your sanity (and your parents' sanity, too) do your share to declare a cease-fire.

To decrease parental nagging, beat your 'rents to the punch. Make your bed in the morning before you leave. Do your chores and homework *before* your parents ask you to. In no time, your parents will be smiling instead of growling in your direction.

Give Grandma a Call

Scientists were amazed to discover that chicken soup really does make you feel better. But they shouldn't have been so surprised. Grandmothers have been making people feel better since the beginning of time.

When something is really getting you down, talking to Grandma can bring you right back up again. For one thing, a grandmother can easily reassure you that people have had those exact worries for decades. In fact, your grandma may have gone through a similar experience, and look at what a cool lady she turned out to be!

Brotherly (and Sisterly) Love

In real life there are no genies waiting to grant you three wishes. Which means your siblings are *never* going to disappear. The best you can do is learn to live with them — and maybe even learn to enjoy having them around.

Instead of focusing on the negatives of having sibs, think about this: There's always someone to play cards with or tell jokes to. And when your parents get on your nerves, there's always someone who understands.

If you think about how lonely you'd be on a rainy day without your sibs, living with them will seem easier!

Here's a Bonus!

In the grown-up world, a job well done is often rewarded with a raise or a bonus. It's just the boss's way of saying thanks.

Kids don't get salaries, so getting a raise is kind of out of the question. But you can give yourself a little bonus for achieving a goal. Reward yourself! Treat yourself to an extra half hour of TV. Or perhaps an extra dessert is more your style. There's always the nearest record store, where that new CD you've been dying for is waiting on the shelf. Whatever your reward, remember to tell yourself how proud you are of you!

Have Great Fantasies

What would make you happy? *Really* happy?

Indulge yourself. Allow yourself to daydream about what the perfect life would be like. Would you live in a mansion? Would you be a rock star? Would you be the one to find the cure for cancer? Would you throw the winning pitch in the World Series? Anything is possible in your dreams. So once a day, take a few quiet moments to let your mind go wild. And who knows what the future holds? Dreams have been known to come true, you know!

Honesty Is the Best Policy . . . Honest!

Sometimes telling the truth can be tough. And the thought of revealing the truth behind a situation can bring on a lot of stress. So you might think the best stress buster would be to tell a little white lie.

But lies cause more stress than truth does. When people lie, their blood pressure rises slightly, as does their pulse rate. That means lying is actually unhealthy!

Sure, that initial lie might get you out of a quick jam. But then you'll remember what you said when you lied. And you might have to tell another lie to back up the first one. And then you'd have to remember two lies. Who knows how far that could go? The stress of keeping track of all those nontruths will make you wish you'd faced up to the truth in the first place!

Have a Conversation With Your Dog
(Or Your Cat, Your Hamster, Your Canary . . .)

Pets are great to have around. They love you as long as you feed them. And they'll cuddle with you at just the right moment. Pets are also good listeners. (Maybe that's because they can't answer back!) So tell your problems to your pet.

Sometimes saying things out loud makes the solution easier to find. And you often feel better about things once they are out in the open. Talking out loud to yourself may seem just too weird! But talking to a goldfish isn't all that strange . . . is it?

Rub a Rock

Have you ever heard of worry stones? They are small, smooth rocks that you can rub with your thumb to release stress. People have been using worry stones for centuries to release tension. When you rub your thumb against the stone, your body releases endorphins, which are natural tension busters.

So give your worries to a rock. Rocks are tough. They never get stressed!

Make Friends With Mother Nature

The chirping of a cricket. The crunch your feet make on autumn leaves. The gentle roar of the ocean. The quiet of fallen snow.

The sounds of nature are incredibly calming. Concentrate on them and your brain will relax. Before long, your body will follow.

Study the Stars

The night sky is an incredible sight. Whether you follow the moon's phases or try to identify the constellations, you can't help but marvel at the universe. Isn't it remarkable to realize that those stars have been around since the beginning of time? Looking at the night sky is calming in itself. And when you consider that our planet is a tiny speck in the universe, your problems may seem smaller, too.

Say "I Care"

It's not easy to be a volunteer. When everyone else is going to see that hot new movie, you have to help out at the homeless shelter. And when your friends are going skating, you find yourself indoors reading a book to a blind woman.

Still, movies only make you feel good for a few hours. And skating is only fun until you fall. But the inner glow you get from doing a good deed for someone less fortunate will make you feel wonderful about yourself for years to come. And when you feel good about yourself, nothing can bring you down!

Call Time Out

It's easy to say things in the heat of an argument. And no matter how many times you apologize, hurtful words will just hang there in the air. They never completely go away.

The next time you find yourself having a quarrel, stop before you speak. Take the time to count to ten. Think about the consequences of the words you are about to say. Is it worth destroying a friendship over? Probably not. In that case, it's best to just let it go and agree to disagree.

Don't Keep It to Yourself

Letting anger fester too long can be disastrous. Not only does anger keep your body tense (ever try to smile when your lower jaw is locked?), but trying to avoid a friend or family member who bugs you is almost impossible. Besides, if you stay angry long enough, you almost never remember why — you just know you're angry.

The best thing to do is take a *short* cooling-off break and then sit down and quietly, calmly talk with the person you are quarreling with. Be secure in the knowledge that you can work it out.

Learning to Listen

Are you a good listener? Or are you all mouth and no ears? Here's a way to test whether you are truly listening. Ask yourself these questions: Do you interrupt people before they finish what they have to say? Do you change the subject constantly? If you replied yes to both of these questions, then you are not really listening!

You owe it to the people you care about to give them your utmost attention when they need you. Because you'd want them to do the same for you, right? Everybody needs to take turns and listen up! And remember, you can only learn when you listen.

First Things First

If you are like most kids, you have a lot going on: after-school activities, homework, chores . . . well, you get the drift. Sometimes being faced with such a long list of things that need to get done can be paralyzing. You just stare at the list and think, *I'll never do all this!*

So you don't do anything.

Here's a tip on how to stop feeling overwhelmed. First, write down the things you have to do — in priority order. Put the things that have to be done right away at the top of the list.

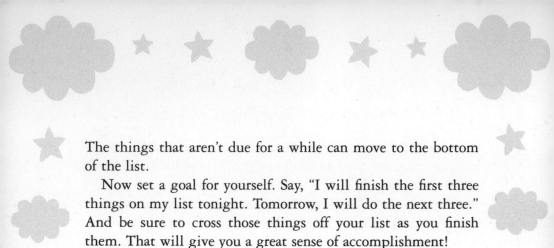

The things that aren't due for a while can move to the bottom of the list.

Now set a goal for yourself. Say, "I will finish the first three things on my list tonight. Tomorrow, I will do the next three." And be sure to cross those things off your list as you finish them. That will give you a great sense of accomplishment!

Don't Let Others Bring You Down ... and Don't Make Them Responsible for Bringing You Up, Either

It's hard not to feel bad for a friend when she's sad. But her troubles aren't yours. And while it's good to help out when you can, don't take your pal's troubles home with you. Ultimately, everyone is responsible for her own happiness.

But it works both ways. While it is reasonable to expect your friends to listen to you when you need them, it is up to you to pick yourself up, dust yourself off, and smile again. Your happiness is totally up to you!

You're Not a Know-It-All

When you walk into English class, you feel totally at home. But when you walk into math, it's like walking into a foreign country where you don't speak the language. Maybe in your case, just the opposite is true. Either way, you'll have to learn to accept a simple fact of life — *nobody can know everything.*

It is important to work hard and do the best you can with all of your schoolwork. But understand that we all have our own strengths and weaknesses. You can't be perfect — and why would you want to be? Just do your best — that's always good enough!

The Land of the Brave

A group of bullies in your class has decided to pick on one girl. They make fun of her hair, her clothes, even her lunch. But you kind of like her. Still, if you let on how you feel, you'll be the next one to be picked on. What do you do?

At first it might seem less stressful to just stay out of it. But that's the *most* stressful solution. Going against what you really believe in causes a conflict in your brain.

So be brave. Defend the girl. You'll feel true to yourself. And you may discover a beautiful friendship along the way. No bullies can destroy that!

Choose Your Battles

Save your fighting words for the things that really matter. Before you start feeling the steam blowing out of your ears, take the time to think: *Is this really worth fighting over?* If it's not, just blow the battle off. If it is something you feel strongly about, however, try to choose your words carefully and keep your voice calm.

Remember: If you rant and rave all the time, no one will know when you really mean it. Save your arguments for the really big things, and your words will hold real power. (You'll also avoid some unnecessary stressful arguments.)

Keep Your Eyes on Your Own Paper

You take one look at your social studies quiz and you know today is a disaster. You don't remember the answer to the first question, and that's not a good sign. But you are sitting next to the smartest kid in class and . . .

Don't do it! Do *not* look at her paper. It's better to get a poor grade than to cheat. Once you get the poor grade, it's over, and you can try to do better next time. But once you cheat, that stays with you. You'll spend hours wondering if your teacher and parents will ever find out. And you'll never feel good about the grade you received. As usual, honesty remains the best policy!

Play Mind Games

It's one thing to stand up for what you believe in. It's another to feel that what *you* believe in is always right. That kind of rigid thinking blocks your ability to learn and grow as a human being. And when your growth is stunted, you feel stress.

So learn to bend. Consider other people's ideas as well as your own. You don't have to give up your belief system. Just acknowledge that there are other opinions out there. And accept that people have different life experiences that enable them to see things differently than you do. When a new idea intrigues you, go out and learn about it. Hit the library, or call up a few categories on the Internet.

If you find out something really fascinating, spread the word. Have discussions with your friends. You'll be able to learn a lot from one another!

"I Love Your Smile!"

Here's a goal to set for yourself: Try to give at least one compliment a day. Saying something nice to people raises their self-esteem. And when you make your friends happy, you make yourself feel good, too.

Try Being Two-faced

No, we don't mean lying and cheating behind someone's back. We mean try to see both sides of the same argument. First, think of your point of view. Then, think of all the reasons someone else might think you're wrong. Being able to predict what other people will think may open your mind to new ideas.

Work Out!

There's no better feeling than taking part in a good, sweaty workout! When you work out, your body releases natural stress busters called endorphins, which calm your body. And the harder the workout, the better you feel. Your phys ed teacher will be able to set you up with some good exercises to start with.

Vary your workout program to keep it fun. Do calisthenics one day, shoot hoops the next. And don't underestimate the power of a good, long run. Running is a solitary experience. Sometimes being alone is a good way to sort out the issues that have been plaguing you all day long. But be sure to stretch before and after your run. **And don't start any workout program until you check with your doctor.**

Here's an added plus — working out makes you look great. And when you look great, you feel positive about yourself!

Be Prepared

Do you panic when the teacher begins calling on people who haven't raised their hands? Does your stomach tremble? Do your palms get sweaty? Well, there's only one real solution to that problem — do your homework!

If you study and do the work that's assigned, you won't panic when the teacher calls on you — because *you know* you know your stuff. In fact, you just may find yourself raising your hand when the teacher asks a question!

Don't Worry About Tomorrow

Has this ever happened to you? You don't do as well as you would have liked on a spelling test. Suddenly, your mind is working faster than the Concorde jet. *Oh, no. My spelling grade may not be as high as I want on my next report card. And that means I may not get into a good English class in junior high. And come high school, I'll be in real trouble, and . . .*

Too many "ands," huh? Thinking like this is called the snowball effect. It can be paralyzing. The trick to stopping it? Stop your mind! Then focus on a positive way to deal with the problem. You can still become a great speller if you really want to!

For the Love of Leaves

Go out and buy yourself a plant. One of the things that makes people happy is the ability to love someone or something unconditionally. But that's almost impossible. People can make us angry sometimes. And pets can, too. But plants can't. They don't nag, they don't peek in your diary, and they don't wet on the rug.

You can water, feed, and even talk to your plant without ever getting annoyed with it. Your plant will bloom beautifully in return. And the satisfaction of making a living thing blossom will help you blossom, too.

I Think I Can . . . I Think I Can . . .

Do you remember that kiddie story about the little engine that could? Even though it was a tiny engine, it managed to pull a bigger train up a steep hill. How did it manage to do that? It didn't suddenly get miraculously bigger. It didn't get over-loaded with more coal. It just thought positively.

Thinking positively can help you, too. Going into a test knowing you'll do well will keep you from getting nervous and freezing in the middle of the exam. And being certain that you are every bit as fast a swimmer as everyone else on the team may just give you the edge you need to win the race. So go get 'em!

"Stay As Sweet As You Are"

That's the kind of thing we write in our friends' autograph books. But how many times have you become friendly with someone because you think he or she is so special, only to try to change that person into someone completely different?

No matter how much you and your friends have in common, you will never think exactly the same way. So rather than wasting your time trying to turn your friends into carbon copies of yourself (which can be rather frustrating, not to mention *impossible*), enjoy your differences. They are the spice of life!

Surprise! I Choose You

The next time you're the captain and it's time to choose sides, pick the worst player first. That's right, *the worst player.* You are sure to give that kid a confidence boost (which just might make him play better than he ever has before). You'll also give yourself a reason to be proud. There's nothing better than making someone else feel good about himself.

Choosing the worst player first has an added bonus — you'll remember the real reason for playing sports — it's not the winning but the love of the game that counts.

Weekly Run-through

It's Sunday night. Tomorrow it's back to school. All those things you were able to push out of your mind during the weekend are back to haunt you. You're feeling panicky.

Take a minute to think. Start with last Monday. What did you do? Did you get up late? Have a hot breakfast? Chat on the phone for a while with your best pal? How about Tuesday? Did you score any goals in soccer? Did you ace the spelling test? What about Wednesday? Was that the day you tripped in the cafeteria and spilled your milk?

Go through every day of the week. Try to remember what

you ate, what you thought, and how you felt. And when you've reached the end, say good-bye to the week that was. It's over. It can't hurt you anymore. Now get ready for a new week. It's full of opportunities you've never even dreamed of!